FIRST MAN, LAST MAN

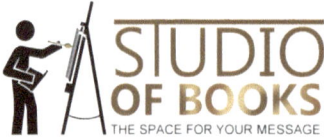

STUDIO
OF BOOKS
THE SPACE FOR YOUR MESSAGE

Studio of Books LLC
5900 Balcones Drive Suite 100
Austin, Texas 78731
www.studioofbooks.org
Hotline: (254) 800-1183

Ordering Information:
Special discounts are available on quantity purchases by corporations, associations, and others. For details, contact the publisher at the address above.

Printed in the United States of America.

ISBN-13:	Softcover	978-1-968491-46-8
	Ebook	978-1-968491-47-5

Library of Congress Control Number: 2025916850.

Contents

1. Title Page
2. Copyright
3. First Man Last Man

FIRST MAN
LAST MAN

World's First Modern Man

Colorful Bushmen paintings of animals they hunted, on the walls and ceilings of a cave in Lascaux, France, about 17,000 years ago.

Introduction

During the long evolutionary history of mankind the first, most advanced human beings, the Bushmen, evolved in Africa. They emerged and created some of the most progressive cultures of antiquity and through expansive migration and interbreeding populated most of the world. They then reverted and receded in many ways back to the dawn of human beginning to a stage of day-to-day existence where their cultural advancements first began.

History

In the early days mankind lived by hunting and gathering—hunting wild game for food and clothing and gathering edible plants from the natural environment. In some parts of the world—such as Africa, South America, and Australia—small groups of hunter-gatherers still exist. Usually located in distant, unfavorable places, they cling to a way of life that works for them. The San Bushmen people of Africa have such a culture and it affords us of the modern era a chance to observe and understand how a people and their present culture are not always what they seem to be and often give little hint of what their history, whether static or grand, has been.

Today, in the twenty-first century, most of the surviving, hunter-gatherer Bushmen live in the Kalahari desert, a great expanse of sandy soil in southwestern Africa. They are the oldest inhabitants of Southern Africa where they have lived for 70,000 years. They are believed to be direct, descendants of the continent's original inhabitants from whom the first modern man developed and emerged.

According to anthropologists, Africa is the cradle of Humankind where some 7 million years ago the evolutionary lines of apes and early

hominids, abruptly parted and moved in different directions. Hominids walked upright on two legs and gradually, as their mental powers developed, became quite distinct from other primates. Africa remained the only continent our forbearers inhabited until around 2 million years ago when a hominid species known to us as Homo erectus became the first man-like primate to expand out of Africa into Asia and Europe. Over a long, expansive 1.5 million years the populations of those three land areas followed such varied evolutionary paths that their early near-humans became markedly different in physical appearance. Some were stocky and strong, others short and slender, but basically they all remained Homo erectus. Europe's became the Neanderthal, Asia's the Peking man and Java man, but Africa's developed increasingly large brains and eventually evolved into our own species, Homo sapiens.

Between 120,000 and 50,000 years ago our African ancestors underwent still further intense change. Whether it was the development of complex language or some other spark of intuitive insight in the brain that greatly increased mental awareness, whatever it was, it altered those first humans into what paleo-scientists call "behaviorally advanced" Homo sapiens. Anatomically identical to us and with mental powers similar to our own, those modern people began to spread out again from their initial homeland in east Africa to occupy Asia, Australia, and eventually Europe. They migrated from the horn of Africa across to Arabia and Asia, and also moved westward up through Africa to what is now called Egypt and into Europe. Over time, they assorted and replaced the Neanderthal and other advanced hominids and became the most predominant human species on earth.

Scientific researchers primarily agree that the Bushmen of antiquity were those first, Homo sapiens. They occupied the Late Stone Age Period in Africa, 100,000 to 50,000 years ago, but were physically very different from the proceeding early man types. They were at that time the most intelligent, technologically advanced form of mankind. They were as evolved as any men who have been born since. In brain size, posture, and in physical development, the eight billion human beings who are their descendants of today have not basically changed the genetical makeup that evolution had already built into their bodies.

These Bushmen became great artists and lived over all of Africa. Their art of rock painting, engraving, and carved figurines are to be found everywhere. The artistic skill, and acute observation demonstrated in these works of art are truly spiritual. By their art, the Bushmen demonstrated their possession of the highest creativity yet achieved in the long course of human evolution. Wherever they settled, they left the world their art creations as they moved from place to place.

Bushmen paintings on a rock wall in the mid-Sahara desert, created when it was a fertile area teeming with game about 5000 B.C.

The earliest evidence of Bushman expansion activity can be found in Nubia, Egypt, Ethiopia, and the Sudan where archaeological excavations have produced many tools, artifacts, use of materials and methods almost identical to the San Bushmen of today in Southern Africa.

Of the Bushmen that did not migrate north into Arabia, some moved south and from those intermixings the Negroid emerged, possibly dividing about 60,000 years ago. It has been generally accepted that there was a similar course of development of both Negroid and Bushmen, apart from each other.

Bushmen are physically distinct from their Negro neighbors. Today there are many different Bushmen people who speak a variety of languages, all of which incorporate unique "click" sounds. The typical Bushman is small in stature, five feet to five foot six, with dry, copper tan skin and tightly curled hair. Bushmen have high cheekbones, narrow, slanted eyes, and slender, taut bodies.

Early in their migrations, after they had become truly whole and highly evolved, some Bushmen moved farther south to the Kalahari and Drakensberg Mountain area and through eons of wet and dry times, some of them have always lived there. Wherever they moved or wandered, they brought the world their precious art.

The Bushmen were practicing elaborate burials of their dead when they moved into Asia and Europe around 45,000 years ago. They also decorated their bodies and clothes with animal teeth, beads, and shells. Their culture was comparatively very progressive and fluid. Their highly developed rock art existed throughout Africa and they began to express themselves still further with magnificent paintings, creativity, and ceremony in the caves of western Europe.

Around 10,000 years ago, Bushmen had occupied and settled in the vast Sahara area that was then lush and fertile, stretching a thousand miles across northern Africa. Many diverse people with lively cultures were also drawn to this region of grassy valleys and flowing rivers. Some had begun to domesticate animals and to grow and store their own food. Thus freed of the necessity for continuous hunting and gathering, many changed their nomadic way of life and established permanent settlements with houses, cites, and evolving cultures, some of which were the first and most progressive ever created by man. Long before Egypt and the great pyramids, cultures in and around the Sahara thrived. At the vanguard of this surge in human activity were the Bushmen.

Bushmen paintings of animals they hunted and sometimes raised, created on a cave wall in South Africa about 5000 B.C.

Two thousand years ago, the Hottentots, who greatly resembled the Bushmen moved into the northern and western parts of South Africa and moved southward. They were sheep and goat herders who also lived by harvesting wild plants. A time later, Black-skinned, Bantu tribesmen from the east began moving southward, bringing with them the practice of cattle herding, farming, and settled village life.

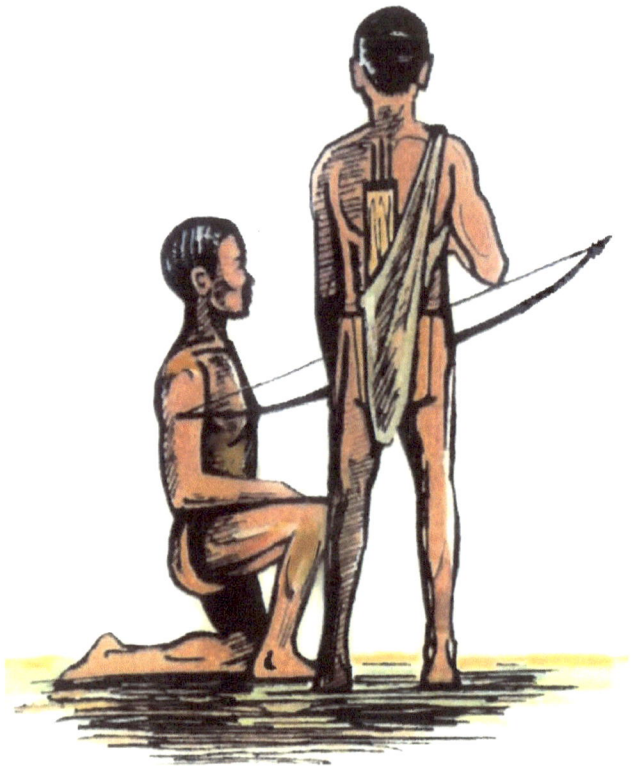

Beginning in the 1600s, white colonists arrived from Europe and extracted their harsh demands for land and dominance, and now, native governments pressure the Bushmen.

Down through time, there was peaceful coexistence and also friction and hostility between these various groups, until today, because of wars, better weapons, oppression, murder, and eviction from their ancestral lands, Bushmen numbers have been greatly reduced from several million to around 80,000.

Many Bushmen have given up the hard struggle for life in the desert where they have been forced to live, and have come into towns and nearby farms for work and to join a more settled existence in the world of today. Of the 50,000 or so Bushmen living in the Kalahari and its perimeters only about 1,000 or less now live completely as hunter gatherers. For them, old ways die hard. They prefer their freedom and are willing to endure conditions of hardship.

Nearly naked, and at a Paleolithic, early stone-age existence, these nomadic Bushmen have long ago refined an art for living in such an environment that receives only 10 inches of rain a year. When rain does fall, usually during a short season in the summer, the moisture quickly soaks into the soil and is lost, although some is caught and held for a while by underlying limestone. Most of the year however, there is no surface water in the dried-up lake beds.

Within thousands of miles of dry desert and arid scrub land, hunter-gatherer Bushmen wander in small bands, a few families in a band, each in its own territory. They live in temporary shelters built of long sticks, bent and tied and thatched with grass. These huts are abandoned when they move on, new ones built when they camp again.

The nomadic Bushmen wander constantly, seldom staying in one place for more than a few weeks. Continuously faced with the dangers of hunger, thirst, and even death, they exist at the lowest possible level of subsistence. Yet they are one of the most humane of people. They are kind, friendly and mingle and trade with the many people, some of mixed Bushman blood, who farm and keep cattle around the fringes of the Kalahari.

During the rains of wet season, grass grows tall among thorny bush and the desert supports a surprising variety of game and edible plants. But during the lean months between the wet season and winter, less-determined souls retreat from the desert and leave its grim heat and thirst to the resourceful "true" Bushmen.

Bushmen Rock Art

Bushmen Rock Art, which predates writing by thousands of years, is found throughout Africa, Asia, Europe, and elsewhere. Many millions of rock art images that have been discovered today were created in caves, open rock faces, and on rock shelters. They help us understand how our ancestors viewed and depicted their world. This art is important because it offers irreplaceable glimpses into early cultures and beliefs, as well as advanced development of imaginative abilities and skills. Some of these creations are comparable to the greatest works of art found in elite museums of the world. Grand, realistic images of animals dominate some of the artwork.

There were figures of humans, and beings combining human and animal features, human handprints, mysterious marks, signs, and geometric symbols. Some experts believe many of these creations (collectively called Rock Art) were used in mythic rituals to control the outcome of the hunt and to bring good fortune to the people and community as a whole. The talented Bushmen artists probably also served as shamans and healers. Some scholars think the Bushmen were shamans

first, and then artists, and that rock art production began when shamans, who were able to access the spirit world through religious rituals that induced trances and altered states of consciousness, could control animals in their wanderings, heal the sick and influence the weather.

Shamans often bled from their nose and felt deep physical pain as they danced to exhaustion as the transformation into the spirit realm took place.

While in trance states Bushmen shaman/artists were inspired by the visions they experienced and endeavored to represent these supernatural dreams in the physical world by painting and engraving beautiful images, signs and symbols on rock, so that others could experience, gain power and inspiration from them.

Some researchers believe the Bushmen Trance Dance ritual served as the basis for rock art and many African paintings found in the Drakensberg Mountains in South Africa and elsewhere show these rituals in clear detail. These ancient works of art offer records into ages past.

Animals were greatly admired and revered by the Bushmen, especially the huge, 2000-pound eland antelope. Images of the sacred eland are very prominent in paintings and engravings throughout Africa. It was the animal of plenty, well-being, and spiritual connection to the Gods. The bison, horse, and huge woolly mammoth were figures of power and respect in Europe and Asia. Exactly, what power and meaning these and other symbolic images carried can only be imagined.

Bushmen painting of an elegant eland antelope, high on a rock wall in Southern Africa. (In South Africa's Drakensberg. Date unknown.)

Some rock art has been discovered deep inside dark winding caves, seemingly hidden away in mysterious secrecy. Other works were created in the open, for all to see.

Black and red dominated the choice of color minerals the artists pulverized and mixed with animal fat and fluids to make the paint used to create their long-lasting paintings. Beautiful engravings were generally defined by graceful line drawings scratched and carved on rock surfaces. Sometimes these outlined images were painted and filled in with color, sometimes not. The Bushman's need to express himself is evident in his many exquisite works of art. The skill and acute observation required to create these unique, spiritual offerings never fail to amaze and create feelings of wonder and awe.

In recent times, when people in Europe first came upon some of the caves and viewed the art within them, they were astonished! In the 1800 and 1900s in France and Spain, where most of the caves are to be found, the locals did not know quite what to make of them. The art was amazing. They told others, but that was as far as it went. Some may have wondered about the paintings but that was all, there was nothing to do about them. It was generally assumed their ancestors and neighbors had created them. A bit later, other caves were discovered containing paintings so masterful, and astonishingly beautiful that archaeologists and art experts became involved.

They determined through their science, research, and radiocarbon dating that the art was created during the Paleolithic period, prehistoric times, in the Stone Age, as distant as 33,000 years ago! They couldn't believe that mankind could have created and produced such magnificent art at such a time in their development. The art suggested a level of probing intelligence in a focused culture that could not have been developed overnight. Yet, there it was… glorious, magnificent works of art—33,000 years old!

Four horses, fighting rhinos, wild oxen Cauvet cave. France. 32,000 years ago.

Bushmen were most likely the world's first artists. Their artistic skills seem to have reached their most masterful stage in the Paleolithic era. Some of the oldest discovered rock art shows such control and confidence in execution that considerable teaching must have occurred over long periods of time. The amazing ability of artists to conceptualize and render three-dimensional forms and bodies, mostly from very detailed images carried in their minds, in their imagination, demonstrates abstract thought of the highest order at a time when accepted belief of present day scholars was that intellectual development of all early humans was at a level just above animals of the wild.

Long periods of social stability was needed to allow development of such a sophisticated art form, especially in a mostly time- and work-consuming, hunter-gather culture. Anthropologists surmise that somewhere in the long, deep valleys and rolling hills of East Africa, the Bushmen people found the time, space, and isolation necessary to evolve from one species into another, from Homo erectus into Homo sapiens and to create their vastly unique culture. In a relatively controlled, tightly knit community, their culture gradually developed, evolved, and revealed itself. Over many generations, centuries, millennia, their remarkable culture grew. In time they began to create images and works of art. They produced thousands of creations. They painted and etched whenever the spirits moved them. Wherever the surface looked right! High on a rock face in the open or deep in a winding, dark, damp cave, hidden.

Maybe the paintings were for the Gods only. Or for the people only, or for both. Much, though not all, of their earliest and oldest rock art in Africa was created in exposed places and was later washed away by weathering and eventually lost. Perhaps they began to paint in caves to protect the artwork from the elements of wind, rain, and sun; and maybe they began to carve, engraving images on rock because it was more permanent and lasting than paint alone, exposed in the open to the elements.

Not all Bushmen paintings and engravings found in Africa, Europe, Asia, and elsewhere are of the same, high quality. But, a great deal of it is; and in general the feeling of the art is profound and awe inspiring! Wherever these big brain, hunter-searchers wandered and settled, they created their art. Everywhere they found themselves, their spectacular, signature cave art, engravings, and carved figurines always appeared, new, fully developed, the first of their kind in a new place.

Bushmen painting of wild oxen, horses, deer, in a Cave in Lascaux, France about 17,000 years ago.

About 45,000 years ago when African Homo sapiens entered Europe as new, modern wisemen, they were called the Cro-Magnon people, so named by nineteenth-century archaeologists after Cro-Magnon, the French rock-shelter where their fossil remains were first discovered in 1868. After their appearance, sites in Europe, Asia, and beyond became affluent with advanced tools, works of art; carvings, paintings, sculptured statuettes, none of which had existed before. They brought their rich culture with them and art began in Europe, partially in Spain and France, beginning around 32,000 years ago. Then, a spectacularly beautiful cave painting tradition began and lasted in Europe until it died out about 10,000 years ago.

No one really knows, why the Bushmen began painting and engraving on rocks and in caves or to what extent there was ritual and ceremony, but the presupposed practice of creating fine art to appease the Gods, to beg their aid for success and protection in the hunt and in life, in an enduring, unbroken art-ritual that lasted nearly, completely unchanged for at least 20,000 years in Europe and thousands of years earlier and thousands of years longer in Africa, is unprecedented, amazing, and incredible!

Bushmen drawings of mammoths, bison and wild oxen. Cave in France, 17,000 years ago.

Many scholars and researchers believe the Bushmen were that first modern man, called Cro-Magnon man, who evolved in Africa, appeared in Europe, Asia, and elsewhere, unannounced and unexpected, who eventually replaced the powerful Neanderthal, Peking, and Java man. And were also the inspired creators of art in the caves of Paleolithic Europe. They brought their diverse culture with them and shared it with all they met as they spread their culture far and wide.

The Bushmen people were well acquainted with the short, around five feet tall, wide bodied, powerfully built Neanderthals who had existed in Europe from 230,000 to 30,000 years ago. They shared the mountains and river valleys of southern Europe with them for 15,000 years! Until the Neanderthals became extinct and were seen no more.

The sudden, departure of Neanderthal populations and their related tools, the abrupt appearance of modern Homo sapiens and the related upper Paleolithic technologies, and the absence of transitional anatomical or tool-making forms have led most researchers to conclude that Neanderthals were driven to extinction through competition with Cro-Magnon or related populations. Greater language competence and higher cultural levels are often suggested as reasons turning the competitive balance in favor of upper Paleolithic groups, like Cro-Magnon man, who was in reality the Bushman.

When modern humans began migrating from their isolated area in east Africa, they were highly evolved and had created the world's first creative art culture whose demand for abstract thinking and visualizing beyond immediate, specific needs, constantly stimulated their minds and made them advanced thinkers, problem-solvers and the first, modern men.

A new kind of socialized consciousness developed. They had invented new tools. Could contact the spirit world through altered state trance dancing. Religion, art full of prayer, animals so alive with life... abstract thoughts, crazy dreams, realistic, stylized, beautiful, seriously rendered things from memory and visions. Multicolored master art created in fire-lit caves, on high walls, ceilings, and hidden in rock crevasses. The fire, the care, the love. Intentions, hopes, dreams. Strange goings on to us. But mind and brain expanding nevertheless.

Did this kind of activity over long, extended periods of time stimulate and excite the mind? Understanding the meaning of it all, caused the brain to develop, expand and grow....

Food & Tools of the Bushmen of Today

TSAMA MELONS

BUSHMEN use light BOWS and
Poisoned ARROWS to hunt animals

SPEAR and
Digging STICK

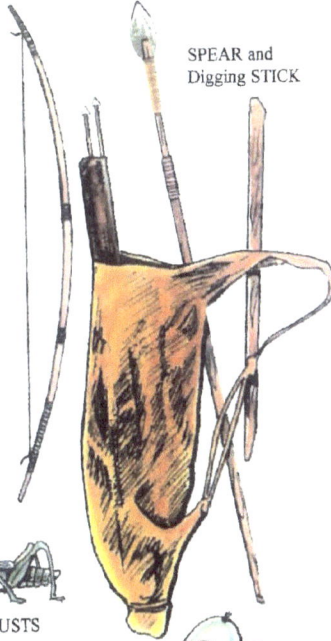

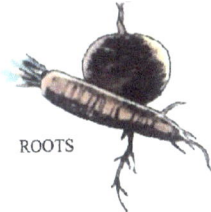

ROOTS

WILD FIGS

LOCUSTS

FROGS

OSTRICH EGGS
Food, shells used to
store water.

Animals Hunted by Bushmen of Today

GREATER
KUDU

ELAND

SPRINGHARE

LION

SPRINGBOK

DUIKER

OSTRICH

Gathering

Today's hunter-gatherer Bushmen do not cultivate crops, or domesticate animals even though their knowledge of both plant and animal is vast.

In early morning and evening, Bushmen women and children dig the earth with grubbing sticks for bulbs, roots, tubers, and gather figs, berries, nuts and tsama melons. They also catch small animals, insects, and collect honey from the hives of bees. Plants make up the bulk of the Bushmen diet and provide much of its nourishment. Gatherers are very skillful and often spot edible food where there seems to be none.

Women and children do most of the gathering and sometimes have to search for miles around their campsite. They always bring something home.

Hunting

Among the Bushmen, hunting is the domain of men. Males tend to be the hunters of large game and are the main providers of meat. Bushmen have no kings or chiefs and they all share in decision-making.

They hunt with light bows and arrows and with spears. Their arrows are treated with a poison compounded from the larvae of a small beetle, roots, grubs, and glands of reptiles of the desert. They use different poisons on different animals, the strongest for the eland, kudu, and the lion, and less powerful variants for the smaller game.

Snares are set for smaller animals, such as anteaters, ostriches, and guinea fowl. Duikers, a small deer favored by the Bushmen, are hunted with clubs and poisoned arrows.

Large animals such as kudus and elands are relatively rare on the desert and killing one brings great respect for the Bushmen hunters. It proves their prowess and worth to the band, since they all share in the feast. There is much celebration and honor to the hunters who can bring home such a large catch.

Bushmen usually hunt in pairs and when hunters spot the fresh spoor of a large, greater kudu, they eagerly follow the tracks until they spot him.

Skillfully hunting the way they have for thousands of seasons, the men work their way closer. They freeze and remain still, hoping the stately kudu will come nearer, offering a better shot.

As archers and marksmen, Bushmen are without equal; an opening is all they ask. When the animal looks away, they rise and let their arrows fly! There is a wild harp-like twang as the bow strings resound and the arrows find their mark

The huge blue-gray antelope utters a harsh sound, bolts, turns, and speeds off as clouds of crumbling red sand follow him. Knowing they would need help to carry the meat from such a large animal, one of the hunters return to camp to get help and together they all track the 500-pound king of antelopes.

Tracking at a measured pace, the Bushmen trail their quarry. They know he is not yet affected by the poisoned arrows by the length of his tracks. He was still running with power and could run many miles before his wounds and the paralyzing work of the poison slow him down.

Studying the smoking tracks of the wounded kudu, the Bushmen hunters decide not to press the powerful beast and pause to allow the poison time to take effect. They rest and discuss the hunt.

As they sit and talk, hot, dry winds blow across the scarlet sand. Winds grow stronger and dust covers the bright, hot sun as a storm develops. Soon their world is full of swirling, blinding sand. Hours later the winds die down and the battered, dehydrated hunters build a camp fire and huddle close in the cool, night air.

Awakening the next morning as heat returns, they attend to their most immediate need, water. There is no above ground water that they can see on the hot, heated sands of the desert. But they know water is hidden, safe from evaporation by wind and sun, deep beneath the sub-soil.

In a low depression below a sandy dune one Bushman begins to dig. Soon, in this dry river bed, about two feet down, there appears moist sand. But still no water.

From a bush he takes a stem, almost five feet long, with a soft core. Around one end he lightly winds dry grass to act as a filter against the fine drift sand, inserts it into the hole and packs sand back into it, stamping it down with his feet.

Then he puts his lips to the hollow reed. For about three minutes he sucks, without any result. He continues again and again with immense effort as sweat runs down his face and back. At last the miracle happens. Water, pure bright water comes through the sucking tube. The hunters fill two empty ostrich egg shells they have brought with them and, after drinking their fill, are ready to continue the hunt.

The sandstorm has completely erased the tracks of the Greater Kudu, but Bushmen are amazing trackers and they set out at a steady trot, searching until they pick up the trail anew. The short length of the stride of the antelope tells them he is exhausted and the poisoned arrows have taken affect. Overhead the sun is high and the day grows hotter.

Brown grass and scorched earth seem to vibrate as heat waves rise and fall. Soon the hunters spot their quarry, walking slowly, barely able to stand. Scanning the horizon, they discover they are not the only ones trailing the wounded antelope, they notice another stalker. Just ahead of them, creeping low, a large spotted leopard measures his prey. Sensing the kudu is weak and vulnerable, the powerful cat attacks!

Instinctively raising his head, the wounded antelope discovers his enemy and quickly lowers his long, deadly horns to meet his charge. Fear sends energy surging into his weakened body as he fights off the leopard's first attack. Again and again the confident feline charges, lashing out with sharp claws and terrible teeth until the spent kudu caves in.

Aware that the leopard has done their work and saved them time and effort, the appreciative Bushmen sit back and allow him to eat his fill. Then they attack, driving the leopard away with shouts, fire and smoke!

They then cut the meat into portable parts. Little is wasted—the skin will be used to make quivers, pouches and blankets; the sinew is used for thread and bow strings; the bones for knives, pipes and whistles; and the horns for spoons.

Celebrating

Loading the great catch on their shoulders, the Bushmen hunters begin the long trek home. As they near their camp, they are spotted, their families rush to greet them. In the evening, after most of the meat is cut in strips and skillfully hung to dry in the shade and wind, they begin to sing and dance. The women gather and sit in a circle, clapping with cupped hands as the men weave slowly around them pounding the ground with their feet in rhythmic steps as they hoot and sing. Musicians

play stringed instruments and a bamboo flute as they celebrate in joy for the leopard who brought down their kudu.

They dance in thanks to the God spirits for their food; they sing to the moon. All night they celebrate, rest, sleep, eat, tell stories, and in a relaxed trance-like manner dance some more.

In the late night, clouds gather, long cumulus clouds pile high like billowing mountains. On the Bushmen continue dancing, whirling and moving slowly, until, from a darkened sky, lightning flashes, the leopard growls, and thunder roars! Heavy electricity is in the air, dim with sudden moisture and heat. Clouds open up and soul-reviving rain pours down.

Way of Life

During the growing season, there are happy days of plenty as various Bushmen tribes collect, congregate and stay awhile around newly formed water holes. For a time food and water are easily found and all is well. But this period will not last for long and harsher times will surely come.

After a period of bounty, the dry season begins to tighten its long, frightening grip. And the San Bushmen, who live in harmony with their environment as their forefathers did, taking no more than they need to exist, must travel in different directions, in smaller groups and move more often, to the next camp in search of food and water. In wet season and dry, the desert is home. They know the barren wasteland well, every hill and clay bottom water hole, every tree.

Because of their enduring skill the adaptable, hunter-gatherer African Bushmen have been able to use the scant resources and remote location of the Kalahari interior to survive. But in the twenty-first century, outside forces are closing in on what remains of their foraging culture.

Past and Future

In recent decades groundwater has been tapped and year-round water is available in some places for livestock and organized ranching. Development of the Kalahari, their last hiding place, for its natural mineral resources has increased. Some consider and perceive the San Bushmen's nomadic, free-roaming lifestyle to be too primitive and not up to date with efficient land use and modern state building: "They should be made to change and adjust to live like their majority cattle-herding and farming neighbors." Many Bushmen have been forcefully removed from their ancestral lands and although some social groups have labored through the modern courts to allow them to return, it seems time is running out. The demise of the nomadic Bushmen seems assured and just a matter of time. Soon they will have no place else to go and the last of the hunter-gatherer Bushmen must adapt once more, this time to progressive ways. They will be relocated into resettlement towns and villages, where water, health, and education services are provided by various, controlling governments who claim to care for their well-being.

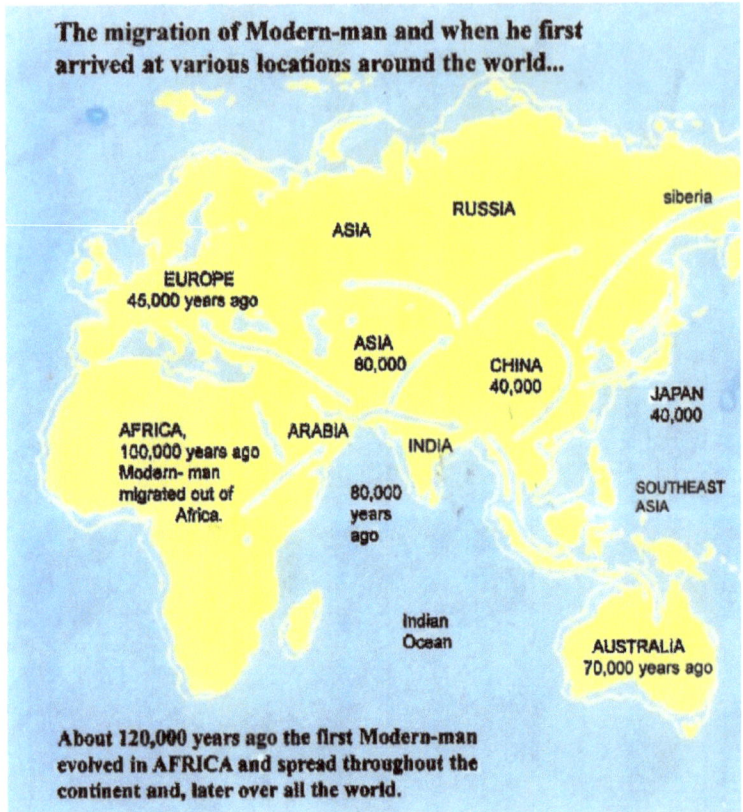

The migration of Modern-man and when he first arrived at various locations around the world...

RUSSIA

siberia

ASIA

EUROPE
45,000 years ago

ASIA
80,000

CHINA
40,000

JAPAN
40,000

AFRICA,
100,000 years ago
Modern- man
migrated out of
Africa.

ARABIA

INDIA

80,000
years
ago

SOUTHEAST
ASIA

Indian
Ocean

AUSTRALIA
70,000 years ago

About 120,000 years ago the first Modern-man evolved in AFRICA and spread throughout the continent and, later over all the world.

Archaeologists studying the history of mankind basically agree that man originated in Africa about 2 million years ago and migrated from Africa to Asia and Europe. Much later, around 100,000 to 50,000 years ago, the most intellectually advanced modern Humans evolved from east Africa and began their migratory route throughout Africa and, exiting the continent at about the center-point of the Red Sea, they entered Asia and fanned out to the east and west. Some also left Africa to

Bering
Strait

GREENLAND

ALASKA

Coastal Route

NORTH
AMERICA
18,000 years
ago

Pacific
Ocean

Atlantic
Ocean

Land bridges
formed during
Ice Age, when
world oceans
receded as
glaciers grew,
connecting
continents.

SOUTH
AMERICA
12,000

the far west and entered Europe once again, this time as Cro-Magnon man, modern man. Many researchers theorize that the Bushmen were that Cro-Magnon man, modern.

The Kalahari Desert in southwest Africa is where the last of the hunter-gatherer Bushmen live today. DNA inspection verifies that they are genetically the closest to those first Homo sapiens, modern men, from which we all came. Their direct ancestors, created the ability to make art in a remarkable, mind-expanding creative culture that encouraged abstract thinking, and made mankind a new man, a thinking man, a modern man. They replaced the Neanderthal man in Europe, and by diversifying in many populations in Asia, China, India, and Australia, colonized most of the world. Cultures advanced differently in diverse places, developing local customs and traditions among widely scattered societies. Gradually, over time new races of modern men, black, white, yellow, brown, and red men, lived throughout Africa, Europe, Asia, China, Australia, North and South America. They became advanced Homo sapiens, modern man, the family of man, the Human race.

A copied detail from a Bushmen painting of a hunter in the Sahara. It seems the Bushmen have always had the bow and arrow and probably invented this amazing tool and weapon. They passed it on to all they had contact with.

The Bushmen of antiquity created some of the first settlements and most advanced civilizations, evidenced by the thousands of archeological discoveries of their signature cave paintings, rock paintings, carvings and other art found everywhere they have settled. The use of a

BUSHMEN: They are believed to have been the first Modern-man. The father of us all. Bushmen are found in southern Africa, have copper-tan skin, narrow eyes and tightly, curled hair.

NEGROIDS: Skins of Negroids range from light brown to almost black. They are found mainly in Africa, have broad noses, thick lips, brown or black eyes, and woolly hair.

AUSTRALOIDS: They are found mainly in Australia, and include the Veddoids of southern India and the Ainus in northern Japan. Their skin colors vary from brown to nearly black. They have black, frizzy hair, wide noses and thick lips

CAUCASOIDS: Native to Europe and northern Asia. They have light skin and eyes, narrow noses and thin lips. Their hair is usually straight or wavy and in colors from yellow, brown, red to black

MONGOLOIDS: Live in central Asia and northern China; the American Indians and Eskimos are descendants. All have flat, broad faces, narrow, slit eyes. Their skin tones range from light yellow to tan.

New races of Modern-man appeared over time at locations across the planet. All of the world's eight billion human beings are descended from one basic species of mankind, *Homo-sapiens*, who evolved in Africa.

similar language like their own, using click consonants spread far and wide. Digs and heaps have produced many skulls, skeletal remains, artifacts, tools, evidence of technology and physiology almost identical to the isolated, Bushmen still retaining a high level of racial purity such as those found in the dry Kalahari of today in Southwest Africa.

In their many different phases of prehistoric existence, the Bushmen have been hunters, gatherers, artists, sailors, navigators, shamans, nurses, surgeons, traders, statesmen, major builders, pharaohs, and the forefathers of modern man.

The history of the Bushmen offers a clear example of how the rise and fall of Human development, so strong and yet so fragile, can be effected by circumstances in the environment, such as dramatic changes in climate or the influx of new people with different cultures.

Who would ever think or imagine that the Stone-Age hunter-gather Bushmen people of today were once the absolute leaders in human development for thousands and thousands and thousands of years, since the evolutionary line of modern humans began.

The Bushmen of today is a race of people as old as man himself, a living, breathing, ancient lifestyle, alive in our own time—that once it is gone, it is gone forever. The Bushmen have been studied, examined, and written about during the start of recent recorded history and their plight has been made public. But they are presented and introduced as simply, Stone-Aged hunter-gatherers not as the forerunners of modern Humankind and the major assimilator of populations throughout the world.

Dutch and English white settlers who encouraged hunting for trophies and sport, slaughtered game animals the Bushmen depended on for food. They also wanted their land and did not take kindly to the Bushmen helping themselves to their cattle whenever they came upon them. They tried to control their losses and nearly succeeded in exterminating their competitive, combative foe. Bushmen have encountered a variety of problems throughout Africa in the past from other Africans and from Arabs as well. They were once a very widely spread culture, but by the time whites arrived in Africa in the 1600s the far South was the only area where Bushmen could be found in any significant numbers.

Though greatly admired for their ingenious survival skills under dire, harsh conditions, the last of the hunter-gatherer Bushmen, the authentic, "true" first man, now living in the Kalahari desert, is generally despised by the uninformed world and by various African groups who have updated their portfolios of social behavior and economic structures and look down with pity on their backward-tracking neighbor. *Why, they ask, would anyone choose to live a life of such low subsistence?*

These are truly urgent times for the once-proud, artistic, nomadic hunters. They have not produced very much new rock art for the last 200 years, perhaps they lost their will to create, felt too harassed, too dispossessed. I doubt if present day Bushmen know themselves who they truly are. In the minds of some, they have become the last man. Once the highest, now the lowest. Once the "first man," now the "last man."

However, they still have the same intellectual spark that their highly advanced ancestors had and passed on to them and to all of us, present-day descendants. Besides, the seemingly indestructible Bushmen have survived almost intact! They are still alive, though just barely. Not as curios to be poked at and pitied, but as a real, warm present-day contact with our ancient history....

Whatever their way of life in the past, today and in the future, may they live on.

And, three cheers to the amazing Bushmen of antiquity, our direct ancestors, who were the first Modern Man. The first Human Beings. They passed on their large brain and expanding mind, inspiring art and inclusive, abstract way of thinking to us all!

As a species we are evolving still....

The Bushmen

Creating masterful art
to appeal to an unseen spiritual power
for aid and blessings in his daily life.
the Bushman opened up
stimulated the mind and caused
an intuitive spark that increased
brain capacity and
made him a new man,
a new species of man
Homo sapiens
modern man
wiseman
with spiritual connections
a Human being,
inheritor of the world.

EVOLUTION of MAN

- **5 Million years ago** in Africa, the evolutionary lines of apes and early humans diverged and went their separate ways. Africa was the only continent our ancestors inhabited.
- **2 million years ago** Homo erectus man evolves and migrates out of Africa into Asia and Europe. First humans to leave Africa. Over the next 1.5 million years these populations followed different evolutionary paths.
- **500,000 years ago** different types of Homo erectus man develops in Africa, Asia, and Europe.
- **120,000–40,000 years ago** profound, evolutionary changes occur in Africa. New, big brain, modern man, Homo sapiens evolve. As advanced as any men born, they expand from Africa into Asia, Australia, Europe, absorb and replace all other early men who had come before them, and become the dominant human species.
- **70,000-10,000 years ago** creative, new rock art/culture develops in Africa. Modern-humans migrate and populate all the continents of the world.

REFERENCES

The Invisible History of the Human Race by Christine Kenneally. Viking 2019 New York

Bushmen Driven From Ancestral Lands in Botswana by Leon Marshall, National Geographic 2019

Stepping, Stones, by Christine Desdemaines-Hugon Yale University Press, New Haven and London 2018

The Real Eve, by Shephen Oppenheimer Carroll & Graf Publisher, New York, 2013

The Cave Painters, by Gregory Curtis Alfred A. Knope, New York 2016

Bushmen Illegally Evicted, by Robyn Dixon, Chicago Tribune 2006

Africa, National Geographic, by Jared Diamond, 2005

The Bushmen in Ancient History, by Mike Elliott, 2004

The Mind in the Cave, by David Lewis-Williams Thames & Hudson Ltd., London, 2002

The Bushmen, by Peter Johnson, Anthony Bannister, Alf Wannenburgh Chartwell Books, Inc., 110 Enterprise Ave., Secaucus, New Jersey 07094 1979

Early Man, Life Nature Library, by F. Clark Howell, Time Inc. 1968

The Peoples Of Africa, by Colin M. Turnbuli The World Publishing Company, Cleveland 2, Ohio

The First Artists, by Dorothy and Joseph Samachson Doubleday & Company, Inc, Garden City, New York

www.ingramcontent.com/pod-product-compliance
Lightning Source LLC
Chambersburg PA
CBHW040939030426
42335CB00006B/197